Caspar David Friedrich

Line and Transparency

by
Jacqueline and Maurice Guillaud

G u i l l a u d   M i n i a t u r e s

Clarkson N. Potter, Inc./New York
Guillaud Editions Paris-New York

By the beginning of the nineteenth century, the Romantic movement in literature, had assumed cosmic dimensions in the land of Goethe. Great changes were taking place in Europe during these troubled years marked by a succession of wars and uneasy times of peace.

In the tumultous upsurge of German culture, the visual arts might easily have been overlooked, were it not for the existence of an oeuvre that subtly and insistently even now forces itself on our attention, inviting us to become immersed in a marvelous atmosphere, both fragile and profound. This is the work of the incomparable painter and draughtsman Caspar David Friedrich. His paintings are displayed in Hamburg, Berlin, Hanover, Stuttgart, Essen, Oslo and Vienna (the Louvre has only one painting, but what a masterpiece!); his watercolors and sketchbooks are featured in collections in Mannheim, Frankfurt, Kiel, Munich, Oslo, Copenhagen, Cambridge and Moscow.

A man of the North, a lover of its wide expanses and its luminous light, and a lover of solitude, Friedrich stands alone as an artist of this period. He speaks to us in unpretentious, discreetly formulated language. His words ring with intense music, while cloaked in the deepest silence; his scenes reflect his innermost soul. Working at roughly the same time as Turner, though unfamiliar with his work, Friedrich sometimes manages to achieve the apotheosis of infinite color that we associate with the English master.

The world he paints for us is not bound by the horizon: it exists beyond the clouds and the mountain peaks. We glimpse it through the branches of the trees in the dew of meadows at dawn on solitary rambles.

The snow of this world is white, its grass green, its valleys tinged with yellow and brown. Yet no weight displaces the water, no wind fills the sails of the ships that glide as if on wings over the silver-speckled carpet or inch their way forward sheltered by a cloak of mist. Time seems to stop in the deepening red of the sky at sunset or in the embrace of the sun that sets the hills alight at dawn. We float through the landscapes full of the dense breath of life and at the same time we are weightless; even Death, ever-present companion on our journey, is but the comforting promise of a future. Man's life - one short life - blends into eternity.

Flight of Birds, c. 1818/20
Hamburg, Kunsthalle

Picture in Remembrance of Johann Emanuel Bremer, c. 1817
Berlin, Staatliche Schlösser und Gärten Schloss Charlottenburg

House in the Forest, c.1797
Germany, Private Collection

Swans in the Rushes, 1820
Frankfurt, Freies Deutsches Hochstift, Goethemuseum

The Gate of the Churchyard, 1822
Karlsruhe, Staatliche Kunsthalle

Hill and Ploughed Field near Dresden, c. 1824
Hamburg, Kunsthalle

Neubrandenburg, c. 1817
Kiel, Stiftung Pommern

The Evening Star, c. 1830/35
Frankfurt, Freies Deutsches Hochstift, Goethemuseum

Meadows near Greifswald, c. 1820/22
Hamburg, Kunsthalle

In their cloak of mist
the steeples, the town,
so near - so distant -
evaporate
over
the waters.

The nets hang
slack,
their only catch

sharp-edged
silver
splinters.

Foam-flecked water
faintly laps
the oars
on the lake - the sea -
here a mighty surge
of cold and tepid
currents,
of intangibles,
hints of
promise,
regret

sails furled,
unfurled,
to take flight
into the
windless
night

sailing forth immobile
prodigy of the weathered
storm.

Forked
posts
tied
together
no longer
support

suggesting
a long
climb,
warped crutches
for the
Giant
within me.

Greifswald in Moonlight, c. 1816/1817
Oslo, Nasjonalgalleriet

Woman at the Window, 1822
Berlin, Staatliche Museen Preussischer Kulturbesitz

The Harbour of Greifswald, c. 1820
Berlin, Staatliche Museen Preussischer Kulturbesitz

Morning, c. 1821
Hannover, Niedersächsisches Landesmuseum

Moonrise Over the Sea, 1822
Berlin, Staatliche Museen Preussischer Kulturbesitz

Mist, 1807
Vienna, Kunsthistorisches Museum

Caspar David Friedrich was born in Greifswald in 1774, on the Baltic coast of what is today East Germany. He was the son of a candlemaker and the sixth of ten children. His mother died when he was seven. Later, a brother lost his life trying to rescue him from drowning, a tragedy that haunted him for the rest of his life.

From 1790 to 1794, Friedrich studied drawing at the University of Greifswald, and then went to Copenhagen to learn the art of landscape painting. In 1798 he moved to Dresden, which would become his lifelong home. Until 1807 he produced mainly sepia drawings, for which he was awarded a prize by Goethe at the 1805 Weimar Exhibition.

In 1807 Friedrich traveled in northern Bohemia and a year later exhibited his *Cross on the Mountain* which aroused some controversy.In 1810, after a stay in Greifswald, he traveled in the Riesengebirge mountains. Around this time he exhibited *Abbey in an Oak Wood* and *Monk on the Seashore* which were purchased by the future King Friedrich-Wilhelm IV of Prussia and led to Friedrich's election to the Berlin Academy. Two years later he visited Goethe in Jena and shortly thereafter his painting, *Morning in the Riesengebirge* was bought by Friedrich-Wilhelm III.

During the occupation of Dresden by the armies of Napoleon, Friedrich lived in retreat in the mountains, returning to Dresden after its liberation in 1814. In the course of the next two years he traveled to Greifswald and the island of Rügen, and in 1816 he was elected to the Dresden Academy.

Friedrich married in 1818 and a daughter, Emma, was born soonafter whereupon the Friedrich family moved into a larger house on the banks of the River Elbe which they shared with the Norwegian painter Johan Clausen Dahl. By the early 1820's Friedrich had become an influential teacher at the Dresden Academy. Even the Grand-Duke Nicholas, later Tsar Nicholas I of Russia, visited his studio; (he would later purchase a number of paintings from the artist).However, in 1824, on the death of the Professor of Landscape Painting, Friedrich was passed over for the post.

In 1825, the year he completed *Mount Watzmann*, he was taken ill and made his final journey to Rügen. After suffering a stroke in 1835 he only produced a few more sepias and watercolors. Friedrich died in Dresden in 1840.

Slowly
rising
from the night
behind
the streaks of cloud

slowly
the languid moon
emerges.

Landscape in the Riesengebirge, c. 1823
Hamburg, Kunsthalle

Faces
bathed in
luminance
by
a soft
caress
brush
against me.

Rift in the Clouds, c. 1821
Hamburg, Kunsthalle

Across
the sky
they
float
frayed by
gentle winds.
Far below
nestles
a tarn
at the foot
of the
rock-strewn slope

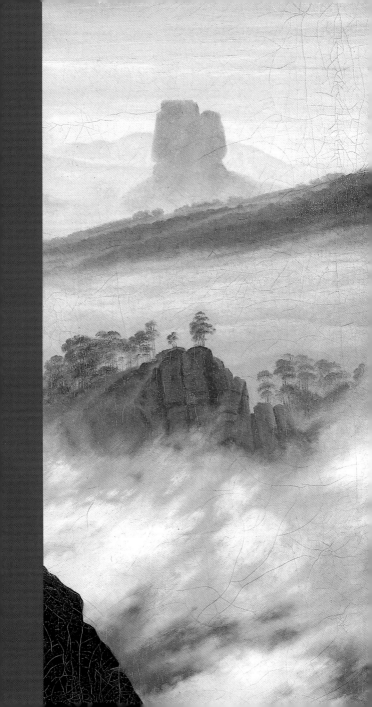

The Traveller Above the Sea of Clouds, c.1818
Hamburg, Kunsthalle

Landscape with Rainbow, c. 1810
Essen, Museum Folkwang

Rocky Gorge Felsenschlucht, c. 1823
Vienna, Kunsthistorisches Museum

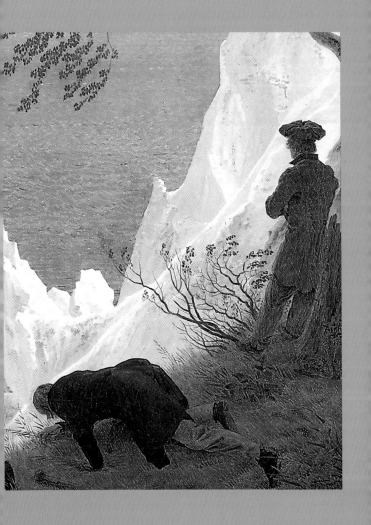

Twisted
battered
bare arms
exposed
to winter's ravages
broken
pieces of wood

frost and ice.

Skyward
under the
powdery
cloak of
snow
the tree
still
nurtures
the harbingers
of spring
certain
to come.

Chalk Cliffs on Rügen, c. 1818
Winterthur, Stiftung Oskar Reinhart

Oak Tree in the Snow, 1829
Berlin, Nationalgalerie

Abbey in the Oakwood, 1810
Berlin, Staatliche Schlösser und Gärten, Schloss Charlottenburg

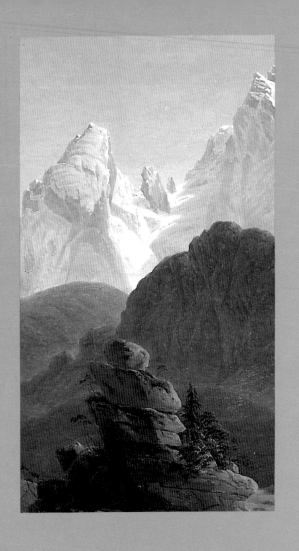

White giant
against the boundless
blue

all-knowing
you bring up
close
the horizon
of my
desires.

The wheat
alone
will not
nourish
the
traveller

The wide
expanses
make him
famished
for
the
horizon.

The *Watzmann*, 1824/25
Berlin, Staatliche Museen Preussischer Kulturbesitz

Arctic Shipwreck, c. 1823/24
Hamburg, Kunsthalle

The Heldstein Near Rathen, c. 1808
Nürnberg, Germanisches Nationalmuseum

View of the Schmiedeberger Kamm, c. 1837
Moscow, Pushkin Museum of Fine Arts

Landscape in the Riesengebirge, c. 1835
Oslo, Nasjonalgalleriet

Two Young Men on the Seashore by the Rising of the Moon, c. 1835
Moscow, Pushkin Museum of Fine Arts

Scarecrow-like
steeply pitched
protecting

against the snow
the crosses
lean
unsteadily

A family
mocked
by
the winds
of solitude
that sweep
the barren
burial-ground.

At sunset
the grave-digger
stopped his work

Black
hole

Lone
rectangle
of
life

Perched
on the spade
the vulture
searches
for
a last morsel

On
the horizon
a low
moon
bleaches
the sky.
Vague
clouds
swirl
above
the russet
land
of
death.

Vulture on a Spade in Front of Tombs, c. 1805/07
Vienna, Albertina

Riesengebirge, c. 1835
Berlin, Nationalgalerie

The Woman at Sunrise, c. 1818
Essen, Museum Folkwang

The Cross on the Baltic Sea, 1815
Berlin, Schloss Charlottenburg

Riesengebirge (six details); *Rift in the Clouds* (three details); *The Traveller above the Sea of Clouds* (four details); *Bohemian Landscape* (two details); *The Traveller above the Sea of Clouds* (74.8 x 98.4); *Bohemian Landscape* (70 x 104.5); *Landscape with Rainbow* (70 x 102); *Rocky Gorge Felsenschlucht* (detail); *Chalk Cliffs on Rügen* (detail); *Oak Tree in the Snow* (three details); *Chalk Cliffs on Rügen* (90.5 x 71); *Oak Tree in the Snow* (71 x 48); *Abbey in the Oakwood* (110.4 x 171, three details); *The Watzmann* (three details); *Arctic Shipwreck* (four details); *The Heldstein near Rathen* (four details); *View of the Schmiedeberger Kamm* (two details); *Landscape in the Riesengebirge* (four details); *Two Young Men on the Seashore by the Rising of the Moon* (two details); *The Watzmann* (133 x 170); *Arctic Shipwreck* (96.7 x 126.9); *The Heldstein near Rathen* (26.2 x 23.1); *View of the Schmiedeberger Kamm* (26.3 x 35.8); *Landscape in the Riesengebirge* (72.5 x 103); *Two Young Men on the Seashore by the Rising of the Moon* (23.2 x 35.1); *Vulture on a Spade in Front of Tombs* (three details); *Riesengebirge* (seven details); *Vulture on a Spade in Front of Tombs* (23.8 x 28.7); *Riesengebirge* (72 x 102); *The Woman at Sunrise* (22 x 30, detail); *The Cross on the Baltic Sea* (detail, 45 x 33.5).

Texts and design by Maurice Guillaud

Published in France by Guillaud Editions
70 rue René Boulanger 75010 Paris
All rights reserved
Published by Clarkson N. Potter Inc. 225 Park Avenue South
New York NY 10003
Library of Congress Cataloging-in-Publication Data
Friedrich, Caspar David, 1774-1840
Caspar David Friedrich, line and transparency
by Jacqueline and Maurice Guillaud

1. Friedrich, Caspar David, 1774-1840. 2. Landscape in art.
3. Romanticism in art - Germany. I Guillaud, Jacqueline.
II. Guillaud, Maurice. III. Title.
ND588. F75A4 1989 759.3 - dc 19 88 - 38556 CIP
ISBN 0-517-57307-5: $14,95
Manufactured in Italy - Bound by S.P.B.R. France